Birds and Bugs

Sharon Coan

Publishing Credits

Rachelle Cracchiolo, M.S.Ed., *Publisher*
Conni Medina, M.A.Ed., *Managing Editor*
Jamey Acosta, *Content Developer*
Dona Herweck Rice, *Series Developer*
Robin Erickson, *Multimedia Designer*

Image Credits: Cover, p.1 ©iStock.com/Falcor; p.3 ©iStock.com/JillLang; p.5 ©iStock.com/alistaircotton; p.7 ©iStock.com/Jamesbowyer; p.8 ©iStock.com/florintt; p.11 ©iStock.com/flyingdouglas; Back cover, pp.6-12 ©iStock.com/Vasca; all other images from Shutterstock.

Library of Congress Cataloging-in-Publication Data

Coan, Sharon, author.
Birds and bugs / Sharon Coan.
pages cm
Summary: "Birds and bugs are everywhere! They are in the sky. They are on land. They are in this book too!"-- Provided by publisher.
Audience: K to grade 3
ISBN 978-1-4938-2061-0 (pbk.)
1. Counting--Juvenile literature. I. Title.
QA113.C627 2016
513.2'11--dc23

2015011980

Teacher Created Materials
5301 Oceanus Drive
Huntington Beach, CA 92649-1030
http://www.tcmpub.com

ISBN 978-1-4938-2061-0

Printed by: 51497
Printed in: China

1 bird

2 bugs

3 birds

4 bugs

5 birds

6 bugs

7 birds

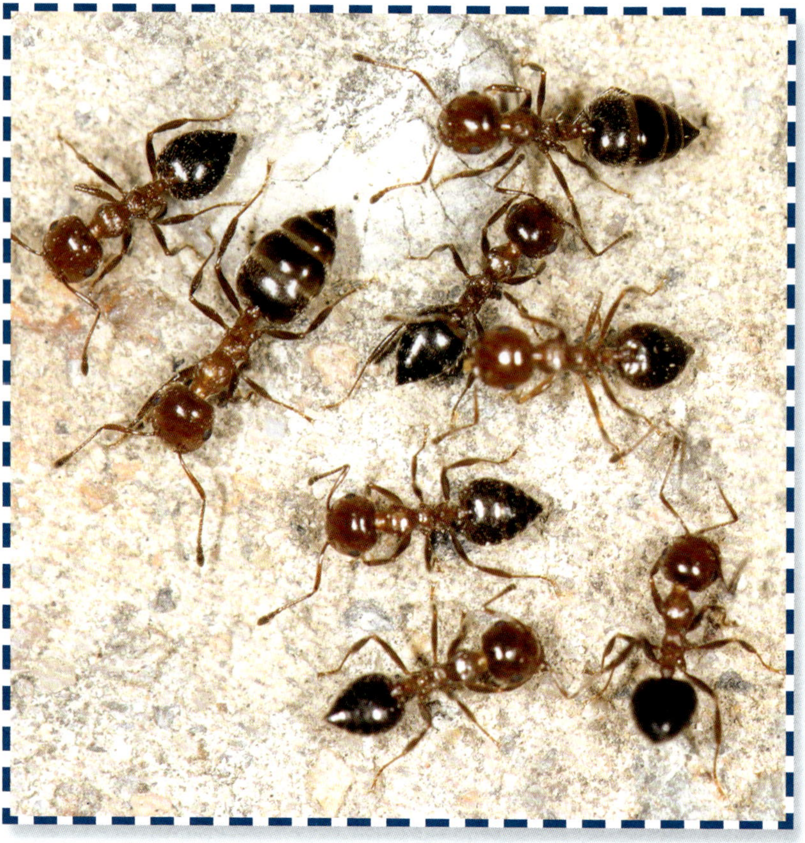

8 bugs

9 birds

Words to Know

birds

bugs